Breathe Here

by Ellie O'Leary

Ellie O'Leary

North Country Press

Ellen – the story began
before, but much of the
writing began at Pyramid.
Here's to our shared memories –

Ellie

Breathe Here

Copyright © 2020 by Helen O'Leary

ISBN 978-1-943424-55-9

Library of Congress Control Number 2019953599

North Country Press
Unity, Maine

Dedicated to

Matthew
Luke
Brigid

Contents

III.

IV.

I

Headphones at the Boston Public Library

The portal was guarded by lions
protecting the building,
protecting the people,
or were they protecting the books?
The three of us, Mommy, Danny, and I
(They called me Honey.)
entered past the lions.
Was I the only one who heard their roar?
We went to the sheltered space of the children's room
where I met a world of possibilities,
at least a few, if not many, steps beyond
what I had already known.
There's so much I don't remember—
not what I wore, not the library lady,
not any of the other children,
not even the story, nor where Danny was
at that moment when I was seated
in a circle of children
each of us happily tethered to
a center console
listening to
a story on headphones.
Made with black, bulbous padding,
too big for me,
they sent a story
straight into my head
festooning it with all
the possibilities of beyond.

I don't remember the details,
I remember the sensation.
Me, plugged into a world,

proudly linked to a new universe.
Passionately hearing words
delivered directly into my head.
Decades later, the first time I host a radio show,
a guest takes my picture, and I say,
"Get me with the headphones on."

I'm Six Now

I should be able to do this
one lace over the other
pull and tie
but the shoe is wrong
the lace is gone
loose so I pull again
on just one side.
I can do this,
I can fix this
because I'm six now
fighting with my shoelaces
but not crying
because I won't
but Mommy hears me anyway,
and says, "Let me help you.
That's what mothers are for."
She loves me.
I'm going to keep her.

The Kids in the Village Asked

how come I didn't know the difference
between a Holstein with its black and white splotches
and a Jersey nearly all brown with a little black on the face?
Where did I come from
that I wouldn't know a simple thing
like which cow was that?
My question was where did she go?
Why couldn't I have my mother?

The kids in the village couldn't understand
how I didn't know a simple thing like walking on the left.
Up the hill on the left, down the hill on the left. Facing traffic.
What traffic, I asked myself?
Who cared where a car was, where it was going?
I wanted to know a simple thing.
Where did she go?

The kids in the village couldn't believe
I had never peed outside. Never? they asked.
You mean in somebody's yard? Or a park? I asked back.
In the woods, they said.
No, no woods.
No mother to ask. Is that OK, to go
to the bathroom where there is no bathroom?

The kids in the village said Momma.
Momma said this and Momma said that
as if every mother was everybody's Momma,
but I said my mother
because I only said Mommy
when I talked right to her
which I never did anymore
out loud.

Marigolds

I went to the church in the village but
Daddy didn't go to that church, said he
was still Catholic. In our living room
he hung a picture of Kennedy,
said he was the first president like us,
the first Irish Catholic, I wondered
if the president would agree that we were
like him, if he met us living in Maine.

On Mother's Day in the Congregational
Church, the Mothers told all the kids to sit
down front. I felt alone, the flowering
city weed among the sturdy country
wildflowers. The minister spoke of joy,
told us to be grateful for what we had.
As the people sang about motherhood,
I mouthed the words. During the final hymn,
the pews of children filed past potted
marigolds, each child selecting one
for their mother. Except me. I walked past.
The Mothers questioned me. "Why didn't you
take a marigold?"
                              I would never say
I didn't have a mother, because I
did get one, but I didn't like to say
she was dead. "I don't have a mother
at home I could give it to. I didn't
think I should take a marigold, too."

Marigolds surrounded me as the Mothers
remembered why I was there by myself.
 "Take one to your father."

                                "No, thank you. I
don't think he really cares about flowers."
I didn't want to take a marigold
meant for a mother, but the Mothers were
not leaving that church with their marigolds
until I left with mine. I walked home with
two marigold plants—one for my father
and one for me. I planted each of them
outside before I went into the house.

Isn't That Your Cat?

The boys pop out of the school bus as if
shot from a cannon when we get dropped off
back in the village. I take my time since
I don't have far to walk and I'm in no
hurry to be home. Nothing for me there.
Freedom Village doesn't have much to see.
On the left there's an old storefront known
as the Boy Scout building, then the post office,
and just a few houses, including the one where
I live alone with my father.
On my right the Bangs & Knight general store,
followed by some empty space overgrown
with weeds, getting taller by the minute,
and then there are the low slung clapboards
of the old abandoned Banton Brothers Mill.
Behind that, the brook that I can hear from
my bedroom if I bother to listen,
although, used to it, I normally don't.
From the weeds in the lumber yard
of the long gray mill building, that is falling
down back into the earth itself, two boys,
just off the bus, are running back—right at me.
"Your cat! Isn't that your cat? It got hit!"
They go back, leading me into the weeds.
Boys never pay attention to me so
I know this really is about my cat
Tareyton, named for the white ring around
its neck, just like some kind of cigarettes.

Whenever he wants to come in our house,
he jumps up on one certain living room
windowsill, but now he's trembling, shaking—

nonstop. I guess he did get hit by a car
but managed to crawl this far off the road
and into the tall weeds.

"That's your cat, isn't it? Isn't it yours?"
I taste saltwater rolling on my face
but hope it doesn't show. Tareyton's head,
most of his body are a gooey mess.
His black and white fur is streaked with pink
and red and what looks like snot. More kids gather.
We all seem to agree it would be best
to put the cat out of its misery
so one boy runs off to get his father
to shoot it, but the man comes, looming tall
over my pet, with a hammer. He's not
going to fire a hunting rifle
right in the village—not to kill a half
dead cat anyway. He hits Tarey square
on the head and all its cat troubles end.
I cannot take it anymore, so some
kids bury him close to the brook for me.

In the house I tell my father—who's been
reading the paper, hasn't noticed or paid
any attention to the commotion outside.
I'm sad, but remind myself it was my cat,
only my cat. My mother died a few years ago
and I'm not over that yet. The next morning
I'm surprised how much I miss Tareyton.
I'm sad all day at school, but don't tell why.
Nobody asks what might be wrong. Maybe
I look sad every day. My cat got hit;
my cat died, and I just have to take it.
I suppose when I get home, my father
will tell me to get over it.

If he even talks to me, I expect him
to tell me to put the potatoes on
for supper, to try doing something useful
for a change. But when I come through the door
he seems almost excited, as if he
is happy to see me. "I almost called
the school." He speaks. "Damn thing nearly scared the
hell out of me." Grinning (He can grin?), he
tells me he heard a noise at the window.
"Your cat tapping on the glass to come in."

Yesterday we took care of someone's cat
or a stray, today my cat is in the
kitchen eating from his bowl on the floor
next to the black cast iron stove. I'm stunned,
but my father says, "Your cat!" as if he
alone has completed a magic act.

I Shot a Gun

Once, when my friend Paula and I
were at her Uncle Wendell's house
I shot a gun. We got to shoot
because he found out I had never shot
a gun before. I didn't shoot
it into the air. I fired it into the pond,
hoped I hadn't killed any fish.
I knew it was a rifle; it was long
with one end of it resting
where my right arm met my shoulder
with the other end pointed
across the lawn, right to the water.
We lived in a place where guns
were common for hunting, not crime.
A handgun might have been laughed
at as a useless little thing.

I knew from that day I would always
be a wordsmith, not a warrior,
figured my aim would be better
with words than guns—
because when I pulled the trigger
my thought was, "Oh, kickback,
that's what that means—
where the word comes from."

Parlor Guests

When I babysat next door,
I liked to know,
as any teenager would,
who was in the house.
There were the kids,
three boys,
and me,
but there might be guests.

White cape style home,
a family, and a business.
The parlor—sparsely furnished
with upholstered chairs and sofa—
was off limits, except for the visitors
laid out in the front bay
as my mother had been
a few years before.
When there was a guest,
I would go view them.
What were they wearing?
Were they from the village?
Did I know them,
go to school with their children
or their grandchildren?
Were they making that noise
as their body stewed
in embalming fluids?
I wanted to be sure, if
they got up, wandered toward us,
I would recognize them.

On the other side of the house
the boys watched
Bugs Bunny and Elmer Fudd
on the sunporch TV.
In the kitchen I got lunch ready,
fluffernutter sandwiches
on white bread.
No one came in from the parlor,
but I had done my homework,
knew who to expect,
knew I was prepared.

Glimpse

Deep at night when the volunteer fire truck
went past our house, firehouse bell ringing,
Daddy and I both reached the living room
window in time to see the truck crank by.
I had woken from a deep sleep so was
confused and I asked him, "What time is it?"
"Why?" He snapped back. "Are you writing a book?"

Well, yeah, what if? What would I write about?
The volunteer fire truck? The deep snow?
How easy eighth grade is, except the social
stuff? Maybe I would tell about Daddy.
I'd talk about how he put my report
card on the floor to read it, saying he
was farsighted. Maybe I would mention
the time he asked me my middle name or
I could write about the time he showed me
that long, deep groove that ran along his calf.
I don't remember what I asked that day;
I do remember what Daddy, who was
from Cork City in Ireland, said back.
"Do you want to talk about the British?
Here, I will tell you about the British."
Daddy was a Catholic boy in Cork
when the British still occupied Ireland.
He was baptized in Saints Peter and Paul
in Cork City Centre, had attended
the Christian Brothers School. As he started
to tell me about the British he reached
down to the bottom of his pant leg. Up
over his white cotton socks, he started
to roll his cuff. His skin was white; his leg thin.

I don't think I had ever seen his leg
before. He didn't swim; he never wore
short pants. And now he's showing me something
about the British. There was a furrow
of hairless skin that started below his
mid-calf. He traced it with a long spindly
finger from the bottom, then abruptly
out at the knee, "See this? I got this when
I was just a boy, from a bayonet
on a British soldier's gun when they came
after us—me and a few of my friends."

I stood deep listening still, as I tried
to picture the old scene. "They attacked boys?
With bayonets!" What a breathtaking word.
"They attacked boys?" I asked again to be sure.
"They did." Then, with one of his rare smiles,
"Of course, we had all been throwing
stones at them first."

I had to make room in my mind for this.
My father had shown passion. He had it
in him. Whether it was misguided or
well directed, he, at least as a boy,
had shown some spirit. And I, his daughter,
got a glimpse of it.

At the Grange Hall

At the public supper in the Grange Hall,
in the early sixties when she's nearly
sixteen, Jane spins around wondering who
decided she's old enough now to do
the women's work of cooking and serving.
Ruth stirs the pot on the black cast iron
stove as she wonders the same thing, looking
at the useless girl who seems lost in thought.
"Maybe you could pick something up and take
it to a table," she says to the girl,
so smart she seems stupid here among the useful.
Frances, who makes finely grated coleslaw
says, "She's done that. Don't worry," as she gives
Jane a bowl of baked beans and sends her out
on her way again into the dining
hall among the hungry people who start
dinner at 4 p.m. While Elva wipes
the countertop she asks Jane directly,
"We'll start the pies soon. Could you help with that?"
Jane knows her mother didn't bake a pie,
being dead a few years now, but she cuts
through pumpkin, apple, mince—putting pieces
made by other women on plates used here
for years, maybe decades. She's wondering
how long this dinner can possibly last
when Mrs. Hubbard suggests she might try
washing dishes. "Can you do that?" she asks.
"Didn't your father ever show you how?"

Jane respects the women of the Grange, she
sees they know how to do this supper well,
but she doesn't feel she is one of them.

She will not be taking a place in this
long line of women. She will be among
women who, like her mother, go away
to college, to explore, to do the things
some people say that only men should do—
like travel alone, earning their own way.
She notices no one has suggested
her brother, a few years older, should help
in the kitchen. No one said her father,
who cooks for the three of them at home, should
be here among the women of the Grange.
When she finishes growing up, Jane will
take care of herself, doing a job named
for a man, a tailor not a seamstress.
She'll be an author, not an authoress.

Ruth stirs the pot, Frances hands Jane a bowl
of beans, Elva wipes the countertops while
Mrs. Hubbard makes one more suggestion.
In this kitchen full of local women,
Jane spins around looking for her exit.

Red Shirt, Red Skirt

after Rumi, "Red Shirt"

Has anyone seen the girl who used to come here?
Scrawny worrier, quick to find a fear,
slow to relax, perfecting loneliness in a red plaid skirt,
things always on her mind, unpolished but ready to roam.
You know that one.

What did you hear?
Stories of her? Stories of her poems?
She might prefer poems made from her dreams
—the ones that travelled with her when she left—
the ones that came with her anywhere,
but she also wants those poems
that came as a surprise
and worked for her anyway, anywhere.
Because she would still prefer life
with poetry, rather than without.

II

Freedom Village

For all the good of it—this
rural place has been something
even less—or more—of a cage—something
else—not a free range.
don't tell me of the safety
or the freedom within,
my mind goes to beyond our

Village to the world out there not
in this very nice place,
long on scenery and nature,
long on good people who mean well,
as I'm ready to
go out to the world because
everything here says everything but freedom.

My Dolls in Black and White

My dolls crowded together
            on shelves
            above my bed
Two were all grown up and, unlike the baby dolls,
            by their dress,
            declared their choices.
Sending me messages
            through the night
            in my dreams.
One in black, dressed in long habit,
            rope belt
            with a crucifix.
One in white, veiled and lovely
            in lace
            dressed to please.
Those were my options—dress in black
            and be done
            with choosing
Or dress in white—hoping
            for more babies,
            more dolls.

Helen Frances Healey Daniel Joseph O'Leary

How could it be that
Even though I was not ready I still had to
Lose you, as if it were my fault
As if I took you out then came home alone
Even though that's not what happened.
No one would think that, would they?

For long? That I lost my mother?
Remember, though, that's how it's said.
Always. "She lost her mother."
Not—her mother left her by dying.
Children should probably have a mother
Even though some are better than others,
Some may be no good at all.

Heaven's no place for a mother
Especially when her children are young
After they've grown, it may be some consolation
Later, when her daughters are mothers, but
Early on, while you're still young,
You shouldn't have to lose your mother.

Days and days on end with just a father
And one who isn't close in a good way
Nor proud of you for the things you do
In school or anywhere at all
Eventually lead to tedium,
Loss of

Joy
Or
Satisfaction
Even
Pride,
Hope,

Or, well,
'nough said about that already.
Less is truly more sometimes.
Every truth has a back story
As simple as it may seem
Rarely do you tell it all as you tell
Your own story.

Odd Duck

My father was an odd duck
which is a strange way
to describe a man who couldn't swim,
probably never tried. My friend's father
tried multiple schemes—farming, logging,
renting a chicken house, veterans' affairs,
finally becoming a postmaster.
My father knew beforehand
such things wouldn't work,
such work wouldn't work out,
no need to try and he didn't.
He was of an opinion
no, not one, he was full
of them. There were people
who had done us wrong, and would again—
the British, the Germans, the neighbors.
The odd duck knew
and so, liberated himself
from trying.

One More

Before Barbara there were none
then they adopted Josephine, too, before
they had their own born-to-them son.
Before Barbara there were none.
Did they really want one more?
Two girls, one son, and then one more,
before Barbara there were none,
then they adopted Josephine, too, before.

Two daughters, one son, one more.
Barbara, Josephine, Daniel, and me.
They didn't live to see us mature,
two daughters, one son, one more.
Even with one, two, three, then four,
it was lonely in our family tree.
Two daughters, one son, one more.
Barbara, Jo, Danny, and Honey.

Why Didn't She Tell?

Somebody, anybody?
Why didn't she tell
her loving parents?
Let's just say
there was only one parent
and he already knew.

When you are down
to one parent you
wonder what would
happen if you
spoke outside
to tell anyone else,
you may never
be loved safely,
may not have a home,
may be put in a home,
placed where no one
knows you—
no one wants you.

Let's just say
he and I were
the only ones
who knew
until decades later
I tell a therapist
who reaches into my core,
as if mining,
and delivers this gem,
"Yes, it is complex."

It All Came Down to Snowdrops

I planted snowdrops
on my parents' graves,
between their headstones,
hoping to make them the first
people in the cemetery
to have flowers blooming.
They never lived in a retirement home
where they could have passively
competed at dinner
about their own wealth,
good works they've done,
their children's success.
It all came down to snowdrops.
For them? Or for me?
Was I being efficient or lazy?
Yes, there are flowers
this spring, every spring,
on my parents' graves.

I Would Ask Where and Why

For my mother, born October 1902, died February 1959
For my father, born January 1903, died December 1966

Hearing that Mommy's gone, God wanted her,
I wonder who does he think
he is, with all those dead people already,
when I'm not done with her yet.
I would ask her where she went,
but I can't because she is gone from life
while stray cats, the lilacs in front,
and even our house, remain.

I get tired of thinking of it, adjusting,
explaining I only have my father
because my mother is dead.
I can't ask him because
he won't really talk about it.

Eight years on, once I've seen
my friend's parents can be in the hospital
then come home, my father is admitted
to Togus Veterans' Hospital and dies.

I would ask why but I don't bother.
I just say ten and eighteen,
natural causes, each of them.
When I was ten; then when I was eighteen.

This Girl

Everybody in Somerville is either
                    Irish or Italian
                    and we're Irish.
Everybody is Catholic except a few
                    are Protestant
                    and we are High Episcopal.
Everybody knows we are supposed to be Catholic but
                    I know my mother
                    said we aren't.

Everybody tells me my family will be happier
                    when we move to the country
                    where things will go more smoothly.
Everybody has a mother and a father unless
                    your mother dies
                    like mine did.
Everybody knows being poor means nothing
                    in a place where
                    everybody is poor.

The most important thing is having
                    a boy who likes you but
                    boys don't like smart girls.
Being one is no help at all if you
                    are lonely or sick
                    of raising your hand.
Someday my prince won't come and
                    I'll go off on my own
                    to see what I find.

Everybody knows smart girls go to college and
                    this one is going
                    to one called Bates.
Everybody has a mother and a father or
                    a mother or a father
                    unless your father dies, too.
Everybody knows 18 is old enough to be
                    independent and
                    this girl is ready.

The House

Even though we called it the house,
not home, and I had not lived
there for years, I never emotionally
moved out of that old place
where I grew up
before it physically collapsed
onto itself. Hearing the news,
I drove there,
stopped across the street,
looked up from my car,
at the rubble.

Good.
I'll never have to
try living there
again.

III

The Zucchini Have Gone By

The lettuce has long since bolted,
maple leaves have turned to fire.
A child may think this season
is the death of things,
when the greenery has gone dormant,
but people decorate with mums
blooming in their fall prime,
plant bulbs for the coming spring.

Fall is the time for planning
new life to follow the present
burning glory of flowers and foliage.
Only living trees can fire up
the landscape in fall,
even if a child surrounded
by the fall brilliance
doesn't notice every year.
One day she will.
She will be in the autumn moment
appreciating it in its own right
knowing she's celebrating
the passing of the life gone by
and to come.

What Would I Have Known Before?

Except for my father's cigarette smoke
and the black coal dust,
      that settled across
      the village when
      the canning factory was in season,
my lungs and I were almost pure.

My young, unknowing plans,
almost always full of thoughts
      that did not include regrets
      about the things that
      had not happened yet,
were free of what I couldn't have known.

Before asthma, cancer, even before
marriage and kids,
      I thought there'd be
      more adventure, less
      heartache but then
what would I have known before?

From Behind My Screen

I don't know why I don't know how far
I'll make it into the exterior world.
What's wrong with me?
Why can't I just pretend?

I can't even ask because I don't know
what I lack, what wall goes before
me as I try to proceed.
No one knows I am here watching
from behind a screen.
Do others have their own mesh wall
that I can't see, that I have assumed
dissolved years ago, yesterday,
or never was?

When I'm here, in this way,
fighting with myself
to perform as if I were not damaged
I prop myself up. I carry on, detached
but as if I were normal.

With My Mother

The last time I saw my mother was June
of the year nineteen seventy seven when
I had been a mother for about an hour;
she'd been dead for nearly two decades.
People were calling me back
but I hadn't seen Mommy
for a long time, wanted to stay for a while
to reacquaint, to discuss a few things.

They said Matthew's here. I tried
to say I'm with my mother,
but they couldn't hear
or wouldn't listen, telling me
I'm a mother now. A voice
(was it hers?) said I had to go back.
The people got louder until
I was there with them.

Mommy dissolved when I reentered
the world of peril and pain,
bright lights and beeping equipment,
people saying my name as if I couldn't hear.
"He's here. Matthew's here."
Matthew is here to see me? Here?
I thought he would be with my mother.
I thought that's what I was doing there.

Holding Up

I try not to think how much it hurts
to want to be so happy,
to be an adorable little girl
holding up three fingers to tell us
how old she is,
to be a little redhead with curls
wearing a dropped-waist blue dress
at her Uncle Dan's wedding.
I love being her mother
but this reminds me how much it hurts
to want to be the daughter
again, just for a day
to wear a dress she made for me,
to be an adorable little girl
holding up.

We Were a Family of Five When I Coughed

We were a family of five,
parents in a tired marriage,
kids on the verge
of young adulthood,
when I coughed.

It was neither a bang
nor a whimper,
not much more
than a clearing
of the throat.

Hand to mouth,
then to chest
and there it was,
on the left,
a lump.

The size of a pebble,
with the weight
of fallen stone
blocking the road,
the lump began

to change me,
change the family,
end the marriage,
and become the
catalyst of new plans.

Pink

I could mention
breast cancer
in this poem
or I could just
splash it with
pink paint,
obliterating all
nuance,
going for
the punch line
even before
the story
begins
to unfold,
then
ends.

Morning Fog

The morning fog pushes itself over the harbor,
blurring my vision just as the day breaks.
Like steam on my bathroom mirror,
even if I wipe it with one hand,
then both hands, the fog does not relent
but continues to roll over docks, over sailboats,
taking them away from what's real
into its thick mist then letting back
a bit as a mast nods or a bell lets go.

In this morning fog, I stand embraced,
like a small island, letting the moist air take me, too.

Gone, but Still

Driving the Maine Turnpike
at seventy miles an hour
I'm only five over the speed limit,
yet my mind is racing,
as I steer ahead into the future,
memory flowing behind me,
emitting as exhaust like the trite sayings
Aunt Catherine shared so freely.

Now she is the one—out like a light.
Once sharp as a tack she is gone,
with her clichés, to the heavenly father
with her ninety plus years of pithy sayings.
Decades of misery delivered
in pointed remarks like acupuncture
to the source of anyone's discomfort,
although more to highlight than to soothe.

The voice that said
"Well, that isn't how I would do it . . ."
"There's no need for that . . ."
"Put yourself out . . ."
(I thought the expression was
"Don't put yourself out")
is gone from earth
but still preaching
in the back of my head.

Say Goodbye to the Rabbits

I'll say goodbye to the rabbits.
The landlord needs this space so
I'll have to move now, make new habits.

This home my writing inhabits
will be changed after I go,
once I say goodbye to the rabbits.

I've grown fond of the wildlife that cohabits
this view of the saltmarsh, though
I have to move now, make new habits.

I say goodbye to the deer, the abbots
of the saltmarsh, to the leaves, the snow
while I say goodbye to the rabbits.

My life had bloomed, where now I blab its
change to all the writers I know.
I am moving now, making new habits.

I think "opportunity" as I grab its
challenge, even though by now I know
I have said goodbye to the rabbits
I have moved now, made new habits.

In This Waiting Room

A middle-aged woman smartly coiffured,
in sophisticated beiges and browns with a red scarf,
shuffles through important medical forms
looks frustrated, starts to cry.
She fumbles through again
then rips the papers into little squares
before she gets on her phone to share
the problem in a text.
Checking her mascara with a small mirror
from her purse she fixes her face
before going in when her name is called.

Next day, we're back.
Different people are discussing
old topics of care, old age cares
along with gardening,
driving, and politics,
names and words,
words and names
can't hurt me says one
waiting for a chance
to talk medical
about something more
personal than politic.

I'm here today,
just as yesterday,
with my sister Jo
who doesn't want to
talk about it,
whatever it
turns out to be.

Shuffling Through

I've named it The Overwhelming House,
the one you left me, with all of your everything
from decades of living—no longer living—
decades of collecting, now collecting dust
here—next to the railroad tracks—
straight downhill from the main road
with its view of, but not access to, the lake
where the airplanes land on water
and the logging trucks go by
sounding like airplanes.

Shuffling through baffles of paperwork,
breathing in the cloud of cigarette smoke
that permeates the house and its contents,
I am walking into the wind widdershins
to my plans at my own house
where I want to read my books,
stacked in hope of getting to them,
as I hope reading for pleasure
will one day come again.
Instead I'm here—where documents
have me bending like a birch
under the weight of snow,
as if my head is caught in ice,
making it hard to write poetry,
while my unwritten poems
dissolve before I get to them.

Nutcrackers, dressed for Bavaria,
now stand at the ready here in Maine;
we put the tallest, at four feet,
outside the front door—guarding
the others inside. A few

would have been a collection,
these few hundred show your obsession.
Cleaning products never used,
your husband's old pipe tobacco,
hearing aids hidden among seashells,
miniature statues of Yorkies
(Is it bad that I'm relieved
the real dogs died before you?)
and vacuum cleaners—
more than a dozen in a house
desperate for cleaning
stand alongside their cousins
the dozen or so electric heaters.
Prescription drugs not taken, mail unopened,
bank statements packed into food storage
bags with their corresponding checkbook stubs.
Medical records and utility bills, all here for us to sort.
Books of postage stamps, boxes of rubbish bags,
piled up alongside uneaten food next to dishes
of coins sitting in the kitchen
with mementos of your travels—
a crystal candy jar from Germany,
a metal bell from down the road
or Panama or California.
We don't know where these things
are from as we keep, throw, or donate.

When I'm done shuffling through
all of what's here, I'll go home
to throw away most of my collected
things so no one, especially my children,
will be overwhelmed by
me and mine. I will address
my things with my new mantra—
When in doubt--keep, donate, or throw it out.

Same Soul

We could ask the river, this river, or any river—
Where are you going
even though you are always here?
Where have you been before
this and what did you look like there?
Did you fall, from grace, over falls?
Did you pool in stillness before your next
cascade then ripple quietly, as you do here?
Are you a river or a brook, a stream, a creek?
Are you coming from a lake—
maybe going to one?
Aren't you the same river here as you were there?

These decades later, I am still the girl
who went up to the pond to sit and think,
the young woman who lived for a year in the Galilee,
who pooled my resources to raise a family
then arose after upheaval to heal
from disappointment and illness.
Living now, in grace and gratitude,
I am a mother, a poet, a friend
whether I'm coming from a lake
or going to one. I'm the same soul
now as I was then.

IV

Six Characters in Search
with a thank you to Pirandello

Crazy Lady In The Attic has the most to say
but no one listens to her anymore, thinking
she has gone beyond the realm of usefulness.
She rants upward toward the rafters about the futility
of it all, the abounding frustration of life itself,
carrying on to anyone real or imagined but especially to

Wife And Mother No Longer A Wife
who, missing her old well-defined identity
with its sense of family, purpose, and worth
wants to be useful somehow so she tries to quiet
Crazy Lady to keep her from waking

Motherless Child who will start to weep
then complain about the word *sometimes*
in the song, as if that is all that bothers her
when truly she has a hole in her heart
that can't be mended even by the efforts of

She's An Artist She Don't Look Back
who is now reminding this cast
she is in control even while they remind her
that is what they decided but she doesn't
always rise to the occasion when needed.

Successful Business Woman Who Didn't Make It In The End
suggests, because she is always full of suggestions
despite all her financial failures, that they have a group
meeting of their mind so they can access the experience

Volunteer Here Volunteer Everywhere

carries in her skill set, but V is not awake.
She is fatigued by all her efforts, by the pounding
of all the demands made on her even though
she was the one who originally volunteered.

Each one is vying while Artist is trying
to lead six characters in search of a focus.

I Am

I pick strawberries,
rake blueberries,
dig potatoes.
I am a student.

I babysit,
work in the school library,
work in the string bean factory.
I am still a student.

I do dry cleaning,
teach ballroom dancing,
work in a medical lab.
I am a wanderer.

I work in a research lab,
do custom tailoring.
teach sewing.
I become a mother.

I sell fabric,
sell houses,
sell mortgages.
I am still a mother.

I process construction loans,
manage a group home,
write for a newspaper.
I'm mostly a mother.

I sell houses again
and again and

then some more until
I realize that
working has a way
of interrupting my very own inside life.

Planning

I am planning,
(overthinking you say)
for all the possibilities
weighing outcomes
sorting scenarios
thinking ahead while
looking behind.

I am planning
the guidelines for
the next phase
or phases,
(you say failures)
I say possibilities,
opportunities,
potent outcomes
of unknown origin
except to say

I am planning for
all of the above and
none of the below.

I'm Walking

I'm walking under the highway overpass,
away from the river. The ice is out,
the water is flowing toward the dam.
Walking in the opposite direction,
I'm going nowhere alone.
The highway is loud, but I am quiet.
It doesn't matter no one else is here to talk,
I couldn't even hear them.

Early morning is for the birds and me
and traffic along 295 making good time
between Portland and Augusta. I could
be there on time if I had anywhere to be.
I'm here alone until a hawk overhead
eyes a mouse in front of me.
I'm walking, seeing the capture and the kill.
I look away, not wanting to be a part of this scene.

I'm walking, knowing as bad
as it is, I'm not likely to be plucked
from this life into another,
even if I wished.

Relaxed

There was no snow
in the air, on the ground
when I left for yoga,
thinking spring is finally
here, or close enough,
maybe I could buy some pansies
for the flower boxes.

On the way home it's spitting white
onto greasy roads as I drive
behind a snowplow next to a fuel truck,
unless it's hauling milk, then I'll be covered
in nonflammable white, bathed
by accident in a snow squall.

I'm relaxed, or was,
at the end of yoga.

From the Bottom of the Well

Once I was lost and expected to stay that way
at the bottom of the well.
I looked up -
without a ladder,
without a bucket,
without even a rope.

I was down in a situation
where there was no up.
None of it mattered.
All of it mattered.
There was only one easy way out
but it was final.

I worked my way up,
building bricks from mud and water
held together with

Desire   Endurance   Stubbornness
        Drive   Patience
Creativity   Dignity   Wits

I rose from the bottom
hand over hand,
brick by brick.

Like a Snow Fence

She won't look like much
when you first see her,
won't seem to be
headed anywhere in particular.
She's scrawny, twisted and frail,
barely holding up.

When you hear that big
voice coming from her small frame
defending her children, standing up
for her people, insisting on her dignity,
she is louder than the wind.

Like a snow fence,
running alongside the roadway,
forcing the wind to drop its weight,
she's just what you'll need in a storm.

Where Were You in November?
For Mr. Ernie Ratten, Mount View High School, Thorndike, Maine

Fidgety Mr. Ernie Ratten assigned a term paper,
saying "Don't tell me in April that you were sick.
Where were you in November?
That's what I'll ask you."

I remember "Don't tell me in April that you were sick."
because didn't I tell you in September?
We're done with each other. That's why I ask you,
because I remember Mr. Ernie Ratten tried to keep us honest.

Didn't I tell you in September?
The class had time and now we have time enough
that we should try to stay honest with each other
even as we know the marriage is falling apart.

There should be time enough
for us to plan ahead
because we know we are falling apart.
The class still had plenty of time

as he tried to teach us to plan ahead.
You and I ignore the signs.
The class still had plenty of time,
but you never want to know what's next.

You and I ignore the signs.
Just as the class had work to do,
we have to face what's next.
I can only ask you now.

The class had work to do
when Mr. Ernie Ratten assigned a term paper,
but I ask us again now.
Where were we in November?

Cat's Gone

Cat's gone.
Took off last fall after a big V of geese.
Must have thought
as he was at the second floor window
that he was just close enough to catch 'em.
Someone said to me t'other day,
"How's that old cat of yours?"
I told 'im,
"My cat . . . . flew south."

Man's gone.
Took off round the holidays after a flock of women.
Must have thought
as he was buying the drinks
that he was just charming enough to catch 'em.
Someone said to me t'other day,
"How's that old man of yours?"
I told 'im,
"My man . . . . flew south."

Spirit's gone.
Took up out of my body,
wandered round my house looking for a place to light.
Must have thought
as I wasn't going anywhere,
neither was she.
Someone said to me t'other day,
"How you holding up?"
I told 'im,
"I'm ready . . . . for spring."

Where I Have Placed Daylilies

After Paula Meehan, "Death of a Field"

It all started on the front lawn of the house
we moved into the November I was ten.
The daylilies came free with the place,
began to appear that first spring, poking
through wet ground. Long, dark green
leaves like blades, bright orange flowers,
petals overflowing from the center,
peaking on the fourth of July.
The all-American lily, each blooming
one day at a time. They were mine
because no one else cared.
They grew like weeds along the roadsides,
in ditches, in fields, in other people's gardens.
I claimed ours as my own living treasures.
There was a magic in them, a life everlasting.
Dig some up, to plant next to the front door
or out back and they'd grow new, yet
remain vibrant in their original space.

As an adult, my real estate career
brought me to other people's houses
with their clumps of daylilies
growing as groups in gardens and fields,
along the driveways, along the roadways.
I found some of my own again behind my house.
Where the new development was going in
I rescued daylilies and other flowers.
Where they cut and shredded trees, I dug up nodules.
Where they overturned boulders, I moved rocks
to transplant the living while there was still time.

The common orange lilies were easy
enough to find but I purchased
bright yellow, red with yellow,
yellow with red, variations no better
than the original, just less often seen.
When I moved, I took them with me although
I suppose, being daylilies, some are still there.
I've moved a few times since— you can tell
where I've been, where I have placed daylilies.
When you take some away you make more, not less,
like using one candle to light another,
like reading a poem to write one.

Irish Enough

Romantic Ireland's dead and gone. W.B. Yeats

The old fella asks me if I'm Irish
when I check in, getting a room above
the pub in Killaduff. "I am." But then
I think of my American passport.
As I start to mutter, "Well, I . . . you see"
he leans over the bar to ask me,
"Are you telling me your name's O'Leary,
and you don't know if you're Irish or not?

In the Old City in Jerusalem,
when I walk into a church vestibule,
to ask about the next Mass, the man there
asks, "What part of Ireland are you from?"
He looks surprised when I say, "Boston."
but I know what he is thinking.
"Do you mean to tell me, you look like that
and you don't know if you look Irish or not?"

At Logan Airport the man in customs
asks me where I came from. As I start
to say I'm American I realize he is checking
all the arriving flights, that's not what he is asking.
Then I hear his variation of the question.
"Do you want to say your name's O'Leary
and you didn't just come off Aer Lingus?

My father left Cork City when the British
were still there. Was he on the run
from Republican activity? Or not enough of it?
Am I American so he could add halfpence to the pence?
That promise of wealth did not come true in our house,

67

now dead and gone with romantic Ireland.
I only know I mean to tell you my
name is O'Leary wherever I go.

When I'm asked, "Were you born here or over
there?" it does matter where I am standing.
Born in the U.S., I could be Irish—
never mistaken for Native American.
In Ireland I am a Yank and would be
even if I were from Alabama.
I mean to tell you my name's O'Leary
but would I be Irish enough—for you?

The Woods Are Open to Me Now
After hearing from my doctor

The woods are open to me now.
Nothing to fear in the leaf bed,
there are no *monstrous reveries*
to curdle my muscle or bone.

The woods now inspire a new vow,
of accepting the path ahead.
Nothing hiding behind a tree.
Nothing seeping beneath a stone.

With no fear in the woods, I plow
on through the terrors I once fled.
The dark can no longer take me
to the tightness I felt alone.

I push aside a low pine bough
with new thoughts forming in my head.
No more plunge into misery.
I know now, I'm on my way home.

At This Moment

Thanks in part to Mary Oliver
I am, at this moment free to be me,
to cast aside the weight of facts
and maybe even float a little.
I'm deep breathing, not planning
not overthinking.
I'm giving and receiving
not looking for healing.
I have no pains, no ills,
no need for cures and remedies.
I do not need to start again,
this time I've got it.
This time I'm me all the time.
No effort to be happy—
no clouds about to storm—
no haze for me to see through.
This is my life, my norm.

Waves Breaking

In Ireland
in County Dublin
in Howth
from the upstairs windows
of the King Sitric Guesthouse
we see waves breaking,
dark water turning to white caps
churning into a spray of light
against the unseen rock below
then back to dark water again.

The waves break
against the rocks
against themselves
they do not break against me
writing poetry in this residency
on this trip I'm calling my victory lap
here, upstairs
in the King Sitric Guesthouse
in Howth
in County Dublin
in Ireland.

Breathe Here

I'm breathing
into a space
that has been removed,
reformed, and reawakened
by my breath.
I'm frustrated I can't do
everything in yoga class.
My left underarm has been rearranged,
my left breast rebuilt
from my abdomen.
I don't see my scars,
don't care what they look like.
I know how they feel.
A shooting pain in my underarm
reminds me the skin and muscle there
do not stretch even if I breathe
into them but I'm here
trying, breathing,
not home saying
I can't do this,
even though
I've been nipped, tucked
and maybe even pleated.

Acknowledgements

Grateful acknowledgement is made to the following publications in which these poems first appeared, some in altered form.

The Crafty Poet II: "The Woods Are Open to Me Now"

The Hands We Hold—Poetry Concerning Breast Cancer: "We Were a Family of Five When I Coughed"

Maine Review: "Isn't That Your Cat?"

Narrimissic Notebook: "I Am"

Northern New England Review: "Cat's Gone"

Off the Coast: "This Girl"

Peacock Journal: "Breathe Here", "I'm Six Now", "Headphones at the Boston Public Library", "My Dolls in Black and White", "The Kids in the Village Asked"

The Poetry Shed: "From the Bottom of the Well"

Run to the Roundhouse, Nellie: "Marigolds"

Village Soup: "Cat's Gone"

Waves: A Confluence of Women's Voices: (an anthology of A Room of Her Own Foundation): "This Girl"

Wolf Moon Journal: "Glimpse", previously titled "Bayonet"

About the Author

Ellie O'Leary grew up in the village of Freedom, Maine, and writes about it from many angles. Her writing has brought her opportunities—hosting a radio show, teaching poetry and organizing a new writing program at an Adirondacks retreat center, and earning an MFA in Maine's Stonecoast program. She is now a resident of Amesbury, Massachusetts, where she serves as Poet Laureate.

Heartfelt thanks to my poetry mentors: Jeanne Marie Beaumont, Ted Deppe, Richard Foerster, Julie Gutmann, Jil Hanifan, Debra Marquart, Marge Piercy, and other writers who have encouraged me including Laurie Lico Albanese, Annie Deppe, Gary Lawless, Anya Malik, Wes McNair, Gary Rainford, Hollis Seamon, Clif Travers, Nancy Tancredi, and most of all to the Ladies of the Lake at Pyramid Life Center—especially Nelle Stanton and Pam Clements.